ARMS CONTROL AND SALT II

Arms Control and SALT II

W. K. H. Panofsky

UNIVERSITY OF WASHINGTON PRESS
Seattle and London

Library of Congress Cataloging in Publication Data
Panofsky, Wolfgang K. H., 1919-
  Arms control and Salt II

  (The Jessie and John Danz Lecture Series.)
  "Salt II basic guide": p.
  1. Arms control—Addresses, essays, lectures
  2. Atomic weapons—International cooperation—
Addresses, essays, lectures 3. Strategic Arms Limitation
Talks—Addresses, essays, lectures
I. United States Department of State. Bureau of Public
Affairs. Salt II basic guide. II. Title III. Series
J.X. 1974P28   327'.174   79-5182
ISBN 0-295-95700-X pbk.
ISBN 0-295-95701-8

Arms Control and SALT II is a volume in
the Jessie and John Danz Lecture Series.

Preface

The Jessie and John Danz Lectures given by the author in May 1979 illustrated "the impact of science and philosophy on man's perception of a rational universe," with two dissimilar examples. The first two lectures dealt with man's efforts, aided by input from scientists, to bring the nuclear arms race under control, a race which science itself initiated but whose course science alone cannot determine. The third lecture dealt with developments in high energy particle physics, a field which in recent times has made dramatic progress in understanding matter on an exceedingly small scale—as small as one-millionth of the diameter of an atom.

It appeared inadvisable to publish these lectures on such diverse topics in a single volume. Publishing the two talks on arms control, however, seemed to fill a public need. This conclusion was reinforced by the accident of dates which brought the final phases of the SALT II negotiations into coincidence with these lectures. Accordingly, a third chapter dealing specifically with SALT was added to the general arms control lectures and a brief outline of the content of SALT II was appended.

This small volume is not intended to be a scholarly presentation of the historical evolution and current import of arms control in general or SALT in particular. Rather it is an exposition of the urgent need for arms control as derived from the nature, dangers, and burden of nuclear weapons and the grave unresolved contradictions among and within the doctrines designed to govern their production and use. The leading theme of this discourse is that society has permitted nuclear weapons to become political tools symbolizing the strength or standing of nations in seeming disregard of the nature of the consequences of actual large-scale nuclear conflict. Only if we technicians succeed in conveying an awareness of the physical realities above the din of largely political discourse now swirling around SALT, will the urgent need for reversing this insane accumulation of nuclear weapons be recognized and acted on. Only if understanding takes the place of political perceptions will we have the tools to answer the question "When is there enough?" This little volume is dedicated to contribute to such understanding.

Contents

ARMS CONTROL AND SALT II

I

General Factors Relating Technology, Politics, and Arms Control

A. NUCLEAR ARMS AND TECHNOLOGY

As long as there has been a recorded history of science, scientists have been involved with armaments. Witness the story of Archimedes of Syracuse. When his home city was besieged by the Romans in 212 B.C. he invented and put into action numerous devices to fend off the attackers. Although some of these military inventions are probably legendary the net effect was substantial in delaying the final conquest of the city. Yet, according to legend, Archimedes was surprised when an enemy soldier came upon him while he was drawing geometrical figures in the sand and he is quoted as having uttered as his last words, "Don't disturb my circles."

This story symbolizes what continues to be the highly ambivalent relationship between scientists and armaments. Science and thence technology have been a driving force in the increasing proliferation and lethality of weaponry. Yet "pure scientists" take pride in their ability and successes in pursuing science for its own sake, unaffected by the potential application of the end products of their achievements. But scientists deserve credit for frequently being the first to utter the warning cry alerting the public of the adverse consequences of the uncontrolled evolution of technology. In this chapter, I will try to outline some of the general features of this ambivalent relationship between politics and technology as it relates to arms control.

The arms race, as I will call the evolution and proliferation of military armaments, is both an enormous burden and a danger to current civilization. Participation in the arms race is shared among developed and undeveloped nations. The total military expenditures of the world consume assets of about $500 billion annually. Of this sum roughly one-half is spent by the superpowers—the Soviet Union and the United States. However, the lesser developed nations are spending steeply increasing sums and their military expenditures are growing at a faster rate than those of the developed nations.

Part of this military spending goes for the maintenance of armies and supporting services. However, part goes for procurement of weapons systems of ever-increasing numbers, technological sophistication, and deadliness. Even if the rate of spending for new arms does not escalate, weapons stockpiles grow, since many of the strategic systems of today remain operational for several decades.

Nuclear weapons are at the peak in lethality among modern weaponry. Thus far nuclear arms have been used "in anger" only twice, when the United States dropped bombs on Hiroshima and Nagasaki. These two bombs killed about one quarter of a million people. Yet the world's arsenals today comprise about 30,000 such weapons. Each of these, with a few exceptions, is larger than those dropped on the two Japanese cities. Fourteen thousand nuclear weapons are deployed around and in Western Europe—one of the most densely populated and economically viable regions on Earth. Notwithstanding these facts there are those who proclaim that there really is no "arms race" but that the present stockpiles of nuclear weapons are simply a natural consequence of modernization of means to fight war, and thus represent a logical historical evolution. As a matter of political reality this evolution may indeed have been difficult to avoid once the first nuclear weapons were detonated; yet these stockpiles of nuclear weapons today represent a qualitatively different situation from that ever faced by man. The total destructive power releasable by nuclear weapons now becomes comparable to cosmic forces. Many of the global consequences for mankind and for the ecology, should a large fraction of the nuclear arsenal be detonated, are simply not well understood, notwithstanding some limited scholarly effort to make an assessment.

Each period of history has had its triumphs and its moments of shame. The Middle Ages combined artistic triumphs with destructive wars over, in retrospect, senseless causes. The ravages of Nazism took place in parallel with unsurpassed scientific and technical achievements. I would concur with Victor Weisskopf who recently wrote, on the occasion of the fortieth anniversary of nuclear fission, that the vast stockpiling of weapons of mass destruction might well be considered in retrospect to be one of the largest blemishes on today's civilization.

Doctrines on the purpose of nuclear weapons have evolved over time; there is a profusion of literature and pronouncements discussing the status and missions of U.S. and Soviet nuclear weapons. A critical discussion of the situation would require more space than is available here, but a few remarks are in order—and these remarks will identify many unsolved dilemmas.

As long as the Soviets had no significant stockpiles of nuclear weapons, U.S. doctrine rested on the threat of "massive retaliation." In other words, under the leadership of John Foster Dulles, the United States announced that it would feel free to retaliate with nuclear weapons against any moves by a potential adversary that it would consider unacceptable. This posture became infeasible as soon as the Soviet Union also acquired a significant number of nuclear weapons which could be delivered against this country. In consequence a number of alternate doctrines evolved.

Viewed superficially the doctrines as espoused by the Soviets and the United States by succeeding administrations and various spokesmen appear diverse and frequently changing. Yet if the consequences, as measured by danger to human survival, of each doctrine are assessed, then the differences are unimpressive. The unpredictability of behavior of human populations under stress, the vastness and uncertainty of the large-scale physical effects of nuclear weapons, and above all the abilities of "rational" governments to control the course of a nuclear conflict all tend to submerge the importance of formal doctrines or goals.

"Deterrence" of nuclear war has remained the cornerstone of each U.S. administration since the dawn of the Nuclear Age. Yet the term "deterrence" is used in a large variety of contexts with differing connotations. In general terms deterrence means that an opponent would be assured that if he initiated war, he would find the consequences "unacceptable." Threatened nuclear retaliation would deny the enemy attainment of his war objectives, or unacceptably impede his "recovery" from the war.

The trouble with these simple definitions is, of course, that they permit a wide variety of actual interpretation. Moreover nobody can promise that the mere possession of nuclear weapons can deter the initiation of any type of aggression; for instance it has been amply demonstrated in recent history that local conflicts using conventional arms have not been deterred by the nuclear weapons in the hands of the superpowers. Yet in recent times some proponents broadened the term "deterrence" to mean that response with nuclear weapons should be sufficiently "flexible" that war can be "deterred at all levels." Such a policy threatens in effect that any war can and probably will become a nuclear war. Thus it raises the frightening prospect that any local conflict might likely escalate to a larger scale, noncommensurate with the limited objectives of the original confrontation. In other words any doctrine of "deterrence of war at all levels" begs the question as to how such a conflict can reach a logical stopping point short of all-out nuclear conflagration. Indeed any doctrine of "limited" nuclear war suffers from the fatal flaw that one can hardly be sure whether the opponent is willing, or even capable, of conducting war by the same rule. For these reasons the basic dilemma remains that any doctrine which threatens the use of nuclear weapons for "limited war" lacks credibility. Just because a credible prescription how to terminate a nuclear war does not exist, those nations to be protected by a "nuclear umbrella" will always retain a residual doubt as to whether that umbrella will actualy unfold when defeat with conventional arms is threatened.

An alternative, more restrictive, doctrine of deterrence would apply to nuclear weapons only. In other words, the use of nuclear weapons would be threatened to deter any nuclear aggression but not conventional warfare. In its simplest form this is the declared policy of the People's Republic of China, which espouses "no first use" of nuclear weapons. Since nuclear and conventional weapons have clearly distinguishable physical signatures there should be little ambiguity even during a war, once the "nuclear threshold" is crossed. Under a "no first use" doctrine the existence of nuclear weapons would do relatively little to deter conventional warfare, but the crossing of the nuclear threshold would become a momentous decision for any national leader to take since the consequences would be incalculable. Thus such a limited deterrent doctrine on the use of nuclear weapons is more likely to keep non-nuclear hostilities from turning nuclear.

These alternate interpretations of deterrence illustrate the dilemma which the awesome destructiveness of nuclear weapons imposes: if nuclear weapons are to be used only to deter all-out attack against each country, then their use must be deliberately limited not to interfere in conventional and local warfare. On the other extreme if the nuclear doctrine invokes their use in case a nuclear power finds that a conventional war might turn to an unacceptable outcome, then nuclear weapons *may* deter the outbreak of conventional war, but they may also horrendously amplify the damage of a war fought only for limited objectives.

This dilemma remains unresolved. In addition an overriding problem with any of the pronounced policies of deterrence is that they leave the nagging question unanswered as to what action should be taken if deterrence fails. This basic dilemma has been hidden behind such diverse doctrines as requiring that, in case of failure of deterrence, damage imposed on the opponent shall be larger than that on the United States, or that in case of failure of deterrence the "outcome" of the conflict shall be favorable to the United States, or that damage shall be limited to the maximum extent possible, etc.

These doctrines cannot hide a *fundamental* conflict between deterrent strategies, on the one hand, and plans to limit damage, or to "prevail" in a nuclear war, on the other. If one party continues to implement strategies designed to limit damage either to its population, industry, or military installations, then the opposing party would naturally conclude that the first party would be more difficult to deter from starting a nuclear attack initially. Thus all this profusion of pronounced strategies in itself adds fuel to the arms race and dilutes the concept of deterrence.

We cannot judge the extent to which Soviet public writings and statements truly represent policy. However those Soviet documents that are available have tended to emphasize strategies for waging nuclear war rather than deterrence of war as an objective. In contrast United States doctrines as pronounced by succeeding administrations have contained diverse formulations of deterrent objectives. Since such doctrines as pronounced have lacked a convincing internal logic, the actual military planning for the use of nuclear weapons has become much more pragmatic rather than doctrinaire. The military services have drawn up "target lists" in case of war which establish "requirements" for the delivery of nuclear weapons against mixtures of urban-industrial and military targets. As a result the designer of nuclear weapons systems finds ample incentive for building ever increasing technical complexity and striking power into his systems. If a preponderance of the targets on your list must be hit after you have absorbed a first strike from the opponent, then indeed you need more and more weapons—and so does the opponent in order to fulfill his matching requirement. If the opponent builds up his weapons so as to include your deterrent forces on his target list, fewer nuclear weapons will survive a first strike, and therefore more diverse and survivable devices must be built. Again, therefore, the existence of such inflexible target lists together with an evolving technology provides a basis for the arms race. Moreover, the "target list" approach hides the fundamental doctrinaire ambiguities and avoids facing the basic mutual-hostage situation pertaining to the populations of both countries (and some of their neighbors!).

The diverse nuclear strategies and target lists

avoid identifying human populations *explicitly* as intended victims of nuclear war. Yet even nuclear strikes for limited military objectives produce enormous civilian casualties through widespread collateral damage and death due to fallout. Large fractions of the civilian population are always "at risk" in nuclear war. This conclusion is a consequence of physical fact stemming from the awesome destructiveness of nuclear weapons and is remarkably insensitive to variants of military armaments and doctrine.

We are thus reaching these basic conclusions:

1. Irrespective of the vagaries of military doctrine, the *populations* of the United States and the Soviet Union are hostage to the maintenance of peace between the two powers.

2. In their most fundamental sense deterrence strategies and the attempt to limit damage in case deterrence fails are mutually contravening doctrines.

3. *Any* form of deterrent strategy leaves a margin of doubt whether the nuclear deterrent will in fact be used; yet *no* strategy involving "limited" nuclear conflict can offer assurance that such a limitation will in fact hold and will not lead to all-out nuclear war.

Each nuclear power should be willing to acknowledge the "limits of power" inherent in nuclear weapons and take action accordingly. Weapons should not be stockpiled if they cannot conceivably be used rationally. While spokesmen in both the United States and U.S.S.R. have acknowledged that the totality of nuclear weapons in the possession of each is not "usable," neither has been willing to conclude unilaterally that their stockpile of nuclear weapons should be reduced to a "usable" level. Yet if military planners persist in proposing simultaneously deterrent, damage limiting, and war-fighting goals for their nuclear weapons, requirements are generated for an ever increasing number of nuclear weapons systems. The sobering fact remains that unless absolute priority is given to avoidance of nuclear war by *all* means—political and military—over the ability to fight one and prevail, then the future looks indeed dim for stopping and reversing the growth of the world's arsenal of nuclear arms. This race will continue unless brought under control through agreed arms control measures.

C. THE PROCESSES OF ARMS CONTROL

Much has been written on understanding the causes of the arms race in general, and the strategic nuclear arms race in particular. Naturally the motive for much of this study is to design means to reverse this trend while at least preserving, and possibly enhancing, the "security," in the conventional sense, of all participants. This effort—to enhance national and international security while decreasing the burdens and dangers of armaments—is known as *arms control.*

During the last two decades negotiated arms control can list an impressive number of achievements to its credit: the Limited Nuclear Test Ban, the Nuclear Non-Proliferation Treaty, the prohibition of biological weapons, the ban on weapons of mass destruction in outer space, the prohibition of nuclear weapons on the seabed, and the establishment of nuclear free zones in Antarctica and South America. Most important has been SALT I, which limited anti-missile defenses to militarily insignificant levels. Yet these achievements count little when viewed against the much more impressive gains in the arms race. In essence, these agreed limitations on arms, however laudable they may be, have only inhibited those areas of the evolution of arms which are relatively insignificant in the overall perspective of the competition among nations.

Man's efforts to control and regulate the deleterious effects of technology seem to operate under contrasting standards when applied to peace versus war. When appraising the safety of commercial nuclear power reactors for instance, risks are attacked by some as being unacceptable if the chance of a reactor accident—which might kill several thousand people—were larger than one part in a million years. To apply a similar estimate to nuclear war is clearly a hopeless task, but few would be optimistic enough to estimate that the chances of such a holocaust which might kill tens of millions rather than thousands of people would be smaller than that figure. The fallout from past nuclear weapons tests has delivered a larger integrated radiation dose to the public than the worst conceivable outcome of the Three Mile Island reactor failure in Pennsylvania could have generated. Similarly, when the environmental impact of peaceful works of man is being analyzed under modern standards, relatively limited impact on the ecology and the natural environment is considered important. This is as it should be, when viewed in the light of experience. Yet while similar standards are beginning to be applied, at least in this country, to military installations in peacetime, there is no question that should actual military conflagrations occur on a scale made possible by modern nuclear armament, any adverse environmental impacts resulting would dwarf past experience.

All this should give an enormous impetus towards effective arms control. Yet arms control has thus far not become a popular issue, although polls indicate that it is generally favored. There is no national constituency for arms control approximating the scale of the environmental movement. It is much easier to mount protests to avert a threat to the survival of the Snail Darter as an endangered species than to avert the risk that Homo sapiens may himself become endangered.

Public perception of arms control issues tends to be overwhelmed by current controversies on the issues of the moment, to the detriment of comprehension of the vast threat which arms control is to limit. The loss of the tracking stations in Iran—a detailed but significant link in the U.S. network that monitors Soviet missile tests—is quoted by some as a controlling reason to reject SALT II, despite the larger global nuclear threat SALT II attempts to limit.

Why is arms control such a difficult subject to translate from an obviously desirable goal into successful action? Classically, following Von Clausewitz, war is a continuation of politics in the relationship among sovereign nations. Applied to nuclear war this doctrine no longer is valid: nuclear war would be a consequence of the failure of politics. Yet as long as military preparedness and both domestic and international politics remain deeply intertwined, the evolution of the nuclear arms race cannot be expected to be challenged on its intrinsic irrationality and extreme risk alone.

This leads me to the question of "linkage" of arms control negotiations to some other political discourse which might be affecting the relations among the nations concerned. Obviously there is always some linkage—productive arms control negotiations require a minimum of civil relations among the countries involved. But there should also be a common recognition that control of arms as lethal as nuclear weapons is a shared overriding interest—an interest related to ultimate survival. Thus the immediate shorter range gamut of interests—differences in ideologies and current economic and political conflicts—should be decoupled to the maximum extent possible. An arms control agreement should fairly serve the interests of each party in its own right and increase the security of both; thus little if any bargaining leverage should accrue if one party threatens to cut negotiations off in order to coerce a concession in an unrelated arena.

To put the linkage question into proper perspective, it is important to realize what arms control agreements are *not:* they are not rewards for favorable conduct, they are not expressions of trust, they are not agreements stemming from a common ideological goal. Rather arms control agreements are tools to limit the threats to survival in the nuclear age.

The matter of linkage of arms control to other issues has become a major issue in recent times in respect to the frequent demands that the SALT talks be suspended unless the Soviets soften their discipline against their own dissidents. This demand generates in effect a confrontation between two "rights" of humanity—the right to independent thought and expression and the right of physical survival. These rights should not be confronted; they are not alternatives but proper goals *each* in need of pursuit.

Andrei D. Sakharov, the dissident Soviet advocate of human freedom has stated it even more strongly: "I believe that the problem of lessening the danger of annihilating humanity in a nuclear war carries an absolute priority over all other considerations."

Arms control attempts, by negotiation among parties having in most instances highly dissimilar interests, ideologies, and social systems and traditions, to delineate areas of military activity which are to be forbidden, while permitting others to continue. Any one step along this arduous path of achieving control thus does not remove the danger of war, nor is it likely in itself to decrease the total economic burden of military expenditures. One has to remember that through its own political process each country buys the tools of war in the face of many constraints, principally economic limits. When an arms control treaty prohibits acquisition of certain weapons, then initially military expenditures can simply be shifted from the prohibited systems to permitted ones. This need not decrease the economic burden unless an explicit decision is made that there shall not be compensation for those systems prohibited. Moreover, the verification of compliance with arms control agreements in itself involves substantial costs.

Actually the impact of arms control negotiations in the recent past has frequently been an acceleration of military activity rather than a reduction. An arms control negotiation, even if only two powers are formally involved (as in the current SALT talks), is actually a complex multi-sided undertaking. Each party negotiates internally among representatives of the military establishment and the civilian interests and authorities. In addition, each side negotiates with its allies in order to make sure that they do not feel their interests are adversely affected. Finally, on the U.S. side, public and private negotiations take place between the executive branch of government responsible for the negotiations and the Senate, which must eventually ratify a treaty to convert it into a binding instrument. The consequence of this highly political bargaining within each side is that many detrimental side-effects often accompany the fruits of the negotiations resolved across the bargaining table. For instance, as a concession to the acquiescence of the U.S. Joint Chiefs of Staff and ratification by the U.S. Senate of the provision of a SALT treaty, it may well be necessary to promise that certain arms, not now provided for in budget commitments, be built up. In 1963, when the United States, the U.S.S.R., and the United Kingdom agreed to ban all nuclear explosions aboveground and in the atmosphere and underwater, the U.S. Senate exacted a high price for ratification. Specifically, President Kennedy agreed that testing in the still permitted medium—that is, underground—should be exploited to the maximum extent and that certain other readiness measures designed to resume testing on short notice in the prohibited media should be strengthened. As a result, and presumably also in consequence of a similar process of internal commitments made in the Soviet Union, the actual frequency of nuclear testing *increased* after the Limited Nuclear Test Ban Treaty of 1963, and few would maintain that the evolution of nuclear weapons technology was significantly retarded by that treaty at all. Therefore, although the 1963 Limited Nuclear Test Ban Treaty had the effect of drastically curtailing radioactive fallout, it has not retarded the evolution of military nuclear technology. As a result the design of nuclear weapons has now reached a mature state: future growth of weapons systems delivering nuclear weapons is much more dependent on non-nuclear, rather than nuclear, developments. This example cites but one instance in which arms control efforts actually had the net effect of contributing to an increase in military-technological activities.

A further syndrome connected with arms control is the so-called "bargaining chip" problem. Arms control negotiations between parties having diverse interests are difficult at best and their pattern tends to be one of balancing concessions rather than deliberate movement toward an agreed common goal. In such a context "bargaining from strength" is clearly an advantage. Therefore prior to the start of negotiations each side tries to build up its military assets in order to be in the best possible trading position if some of these weapons have to be limited or given away during the negotiatons. As a consequnce, some very dubious or premature military procurement decisions tend to be made, driven by the argument that we should have something to give away at the bargaining table in a future arms control negotiation.

A historical case in point stems from the ABM debate of the late 1960s. Here the intrinsic technical merit of deploying a defense against incoming ballistic missiles was hotly contested in the Congress. The argument which proved decisive for Senate approval by the smallest of margins was that the ABM was needed to give bargaining strength at the negotiating table with the Soviets in the forthcoming SALT I discussions. Clearly, similar reasoning must have been playing a role on the Soviet side. In fact the Soviets are facing a particular problem in this respect: traditionally the West has been leading the Soviet Union in the *quality* of military technology. Therefore when arms control negotiations take place the Soviets are generally intransigent against freezing by treaty technology in those areas in which they are lagging. In other words the imminence of arms control negotiations provides an internal argument by military interests to bolster their technology to the maximum extent possible lest future arms control agreements lock them in a position of inferior technology.

Thus the dynamics of arms control negotiations, the overriding shared interest in survival in the nuclear age notwithstanding, can in itself accelerate military expansion, unless the negotiations and their context are carefully managed. However, there is another and possibly even more significant impact of arms control negotiations on the buildup of weapons. This stems from the public attention focused by controversial arms control negotiations on the *perceived* relative military strength of nations. It is commonplace to relate a nation's international political leverage to its military strength. The difficulty with the use of military power in such a political context is that it is not the *reality* of military strength and the *actual* potential performance of men and their military equipment which is important, but the *perception* of the parties of their military strength.

Unfortunately during the last decades spokesmen, particularly in the United States, have engaged in what one might aptly call "negative salesmanship" in respect to their military strength. We can read daily about the growing threat of the opponent and the increasing gaps in various selected armaments, be it a missile gap, civil defense gap, throw-weight gap, or whatever "gap" one wishes to name. The purpose of such negative salesmanship is generally not to accuse the opponent of excessive aggressiveness, but rather to influence the domestic decision makers towards greater generosity in providing military hardware. However, such a campaign generates adverse effects. Obviously if it is repeated strongly enough that the United States is unable to deter future conflict, let alone prevail in it, such assertions will become credible in time and confidence in the United States will deteriorate. Indeed with deterrence of nuclear war being the primary objective of nuclear weapons, such proclamations of military weakness might become self-fulfilling prophecies. *Deterrence is a state of mind* of national leaders—influenced by many factors—and not an objective technical situation.

Unbalanced and selective assertions of military

weakness naturally draw counter-assertions emphasizing our military strength and those technological achievements where the United States is clearly ahead. But such an emphasis on selected items of military strength can sound like "saber-rattling" or outright threat to the opponent. Thus we see the roots of a battle between arms controller and military spender for the political perception of military strength. This contest tends to submerge the technical reality of nuclear weapons and the potential disaster which nuclear war would bring to the world. In other words, as the debate on nuclear weapons proceeds without adequate regard for the physical realities and, more important, the physical uncertainties inherent in the actual use of nuclear weaponry, then the nations involved tend to lose any meaningful mechanism to answer the question "When is enough enough?"

II

Specific Issues
in the Science and Politics
of Arms Control

A. PERCEPTION VERSUS TECHNICAL REALITY

In the last chapter I cited as a factor impeding the achievement of meaningful arms control that nuclear weapons have largely become symbols of such diverse qualities as inferiority or superiority, national resolve, or just the power status of a nation. Yet few, if any, instances of controversy among nations, when analyzed with deserved skepticism, would justify the extreme risks inherent in the use of nuclear weapons to resolve the conflict. No cases of diverging national interests are so great as to warrant the price of all-out nuclear war. Nuclear weapons have, as much as any instruments of power, given a dramatic demonstration of the limits of such power. As saner heads prevailed against counsel to use nuclear weapons for limited objectives in Korea and in Vietnam, the conclusion was reached that the short-range advantage of their use cannot outweigh their long-range impact and threat of escalation, and consequent wholesale destruction.

Yet the fact remains that nuclear weapons are generally viewed in a primarily political, not physical, context, and this has been the dominant difficulty in arriving at reasonable arms control agreements. When weapons are viewed as physical tools, then natural limits apply: if a high-value target is to be killed, it makes no sense to kill it over and over again. Thus at most very few weapons should be aimed at each important target and further weapons are aimed at targets of progressively lesser value. As a result of the vast stockpiles of nuclear weapons this process results in "target lists" containing items of marginal value at best. If nations engage in a contest, which might even be called a "potlatch," to accumulate nuclear weapons for political ends, then there no longer exists a natural mechanism to indicate when the limits of militarily useful or even usable power have been reached.

As indicated in the previous chapter, unfortunately the very mechanism of arms control negotiations and the processes of public debate in our society have aggravated the situation. Few senators would dare to defend a position in which the opponent in an arms control agreement, say, is permitted to have 8,732 objects of war, while the United States has agreed to settle for 6,224 for our own force. Yet, there may well be good reasons to settle for inequality if other factors pertain which tend to offset that inequality but which cannot be described by simple numbers. For instance, in comparing the United States and the Soviet Union, one has to take into account that the U.S.S.R. has to deal with more than one unfriendly frontier, while the United States only faces its potential enemies overseas. In dealing with ships and submarines, one has to take into account that different nations have different levels of access to ocean areas and to secure harbors. Thus, debating pure numbers as an indication as to "who is ahead and behind" can become unproductive or outright destructive because it lends itself to demagoguery through gross oversimplification.

This issue has come to the forefront in connection with current SALT debates. Those who like to emphasize Soviet superiority recite numerical indices in which the Soviets are ahead strategically, such as the total number of land-based missiles and the "throw-weight" they carry. Those that like to emphasize the secure nature of the U.S. position describe our technical lead, our advanced research and development in cruise missiles, the superior numbers and qualities of our MIRVed missiles carried by the U.S. submarines at sea, and our current numerical superiority measured in numbers of individual nuclear weapons which can be rained on an enemy in retaliation.

None of this has much meaning out of the context of the total strategic position of the two countries. The actual outcome of a battle involving nuclear weapons depends upon an enormous number of factors which cannot be determined by such simplistic numbers. As in many military matters, the human element is a large factor in defining how a conflict would actually evolve. Those who demand certainty of performance and reliability in military weapons tend not to acknowledge the least reliable and predictable component of military conflict, which is *man*. Nowhere is this inconsistency more evident than in most discussion concerning nuclear war. No fixed doctrine and no computer calculation can describe what a President or lower-echelon commander would actually do once nuclear weapons have been used at all. New Achilles' heels keep being discovered in the system of command and control which is the common element needed to execute an actual decision for use of nuclear weapons.

This blatant inconsistency is coming to the fore-front again in the current debates about the comprehensive nuclear test ban. Here the opponents of a comprehensive nuclear test ban are expressing concern that even over a time span as short as five or even three years the reliability of our nuclear stockpile would deteriorate to unacceptable values. Yet nuclear test experience of the past has shown that such fears are unwarranted. Nuclear tests dedicated solely to check the performance of weapons in the stockpile have only very rarely been carried out. Non-nuclear inspections and tests have sufficed to identify defects. As long as nuclear tests have been permitted, such defects can either be corrected by redesign (which generally requires nuclear tests) or repair and replacement (which generally does not).

A very large majority of tests, most of which involved new designs, have worked as predicted. Thus those who worry about the unreliability of the stockpile, should a comprehensive nuclear test ban be successfully negotiated, are invoking a discontinuity with past history and are demanding much more stringent limits on reliability of nuclear warheads than they ask of the other components of military systems, let alone the human links. When faced with this argument, the response frequently shifts to the perceptual arena: "Yes, we know that on purely technical grounds reliability is most likely adequate, but if there were no testing, then our nuclear weapons will be *perceived* as being unreliable." Again, we are facing a situation where the shift of argument from reasoning based on physical reality to a perceptual problem tends to pull the rug out from under any rational substantive discourse.

B. THE NEUTRON BOMB

Let me illustrate this general situation with a concrete example. This is the so-called "neutron bomb." In the next chapter we will discuss SALT, which is also replete with examples of conflicts between perception and reality.

All nuclear weapons kill through blast, heat, radiation, radioactive fallout, and post-attack consequences, such as fire, sickness, epidemics, and lack of life's necessities. In the absence of any negotiated controls on the evolution of nuclear weapons technology, such weapons have been developed for a large number of purposes and exhibiting a large number of characteristics. There are weapons primarily designed for "strategic" use, where generally large explosive power packaged in small volume is essential, and where the special conditions involved in delivery by missile or bomb must be considered in the design. Then, there are weapons designed for "tactical" use, which are designed to offer special characteristics believed advantageous over conventional arms for specific battlefield situations. Thus, nuclear weapons differ in their total explosive power as well as in the mixture of their lethal effects, and in their packaging for the intended application.

In recent times, U.S. and Soviet nuclear weapons laboratories have engaged in what one might call product adaptation and diversification. The technology of nuclear weapons is mature; there has not been any recent breakthrough in nuclear weapons development. Rather, the mixture of desired effects has been optimized for various military purposes. Efficiencies in terms of the ratio of explosive yield to weight, physical size, and control mechanisms have been improved.

The public furor surrounding the neutron bomb therefore appears surprising. This weapon has been hailed by its proponents as a "breakthrough" in U.S. technology in conducting tactical war, while it has been decried as a threat to peace by its opponents. Yet, if the neutron bomb is a product of specialization rather than a conceptual innovation, then how can it make such a large qualitative difference in warfare? The correct answer is that in fact it does no such thing, and it is only the existence of the public furor that has given the neutron bomb such large political importance.

Currently the United States has more than 7,000 nuclear weapons stationed in Western Europe and there have been relatively few changes in their characteristics during the last decade. This circumstance reflects more the priorities which the United States has given to the development of such weapons than it does the stagnation of tactical nuclear weapons technology; priority has been given to strategic rather than tactical nuclear weapons development. This priority derives from two factors: (1) the increasing competition between the United States and the U.S.S.R. in the strategic field and the development of a variety of strategic delivery systems, generally designed with new nuclear devices, and (2) the still-continuing vacillation and debate associated with the mission and utility of tactical nuclear weapons. In recent times, however, modernization programs for tactical weapons have been undertaken by the weapons laboratories. One of these is the W-70-MOD3 warhead for the Lance missile which was designated in the open congressional budget submittal as an "enhanced radiation warhead." This terminology caught the eye of an enterprising *Washington Post* reporter and, in turn, excited some of the congressional staff. This "enhanced radiation" designation connected this development in the minds of critics of nuclear weapons with the "neutron bomb" which had played a large role in the controversies surrounding the nuclear test ban negotiations in the early 1960s.

In 1963, a Limited Nuclear Test Ban Treaty (LTBT) was enacted which forbade nuclear tests in the atmosphere, outer space, and underwater, but permitted continued testing underground. This treaty was a retreat from the goal of a comprehensive nuclear test ban treaty (CTBT) which would stop *all* nuclear testing. This retreat proved necessary since there was opposition by the Soviets to highly intrusive inspection, but there was also much opposition then, as there is today, to a CTBT from the U.S. weapons laboratories and from military and other spokesmen. It is of course likely that there was also similar opposition within the Soviet establishment.

In the era before 1963 one of the most publicized arguments in the United States was that a comprehensive nuclear test ban treaty would prevent the development of a so-called "neutron bomb." This was then identified as a "clean device," that is, a pure fusion weapon eliminating the need for any fission component, and therefore not producing any residual fission-product radioactivity. As was vociferously expounded by, among others, the late Senator Dodd of Connecticut, the principal danger of a comprehensive test ban treaty to the security of this nation was said to be that the Soviets might develop such a device clandestinely, while the United States would be prevented from pursuing such a course. It is interesting to note that the dominant reason for opposing a CTBT has been a different one each time the CTBT debate has been revived.

Actually, in retrospect, most would agree that U.S. security would have been greater today had a comprehensive, rather than a limited, test ban been negotiated in 1963. At that time U.S. nuclear technology was definitely more advanced relative to the Soviets than is the case today. A comprehensive test ban would have tended to preserve that status.

The arguments for the military utility of a neutron bomb were brought forth by numerous military analysts, particularly S. T. Cohen, then at the Rand Corporation. The argument went somewhat as follows: A pure fusion device would emit a copious amount of 14 MeV neutrons but would leave no radioactive fission products. The radius at which the blast of a pure fusion device of moderate yield would be lethal would be relatively small, at least against people enjoying some form of blast protection. On the other hand, 14 MeV neutrons are highly penetrating: their intensity is reduced by only a factor of two after penetrating a foot or so of earth or masonry, and is only slightly affected by the thickness of steel apt to be encountered in armored vehicles. The intensity of these neutrons falls off rather sharply with distance. Therefore Cohen and others postulated that within a well-defined radius of a neutron bomb explosion most people would be killed by neutron radiation, while within that radius structures would be relatively unharmed and radioactive contamination would be minimal. Outside that lethal radius both people and structures would be essentially unscathed. Therefore the damage caused in a nuclear battle could be well circumscribed and reentry by victorious troops could be accomplished in short order.

This simplified picture of the efficacy even of a conceptually idealized neutron bomb is a gross oversimplification of the actual physical circumstances.

First, we must recognize that a pure fusion device has never been developed and all devices currently under development have a powerful fission component. Moreover, neutrons produce radioactivity in themselves since, when ultimately absorbed, they activate almost all materials and this leads to substantial radioactivity, although to a much lesser extent than might be encountered by the actual deposition of fission products.

Second, the blast damage by a neutron bomb is not at all negligible; there is no way to release energies in the kiloton range without at the same time producing a major blast. All that a neutron bomb can do is to increase the *relative* lethality by neutron radiation compared to that of the blast.

Third, the use of neutron radiation as a weapon introduces peculiar uncertainties of its own. The dosage received depends on both the distance from the blast and the obstacles in the path of the radiation, such as changes in terrain and massive structures. Moreover, the so-called "mean lethal dose" (450 rads) at which half of the victims will eventually succumb would not in general result in death until approximately two weeks had passed. A dose required to disable a victim instantaneously would be somewhat below 10,000 rads. Therefore the sharp radius of lethality which was postulated by the protagonists of neutron weapons to permit close engagement and quick reentry by the attacking troops is simply not real.

Most important of all, one must recognize that all these considerations are based on idealized physical models in which it is assumed that the nuclear weapons will be delivered with pinpoint accuracy and without targeting errors. If one examines the statistics on battlefield errors (resulting even at times in fire on friendly troops) as actually recorded in World War II, Korea, and Vietnam, then one recognizes that the "cookie cutter" type of tactical nuclear war envisaged by Cohen and others is a macabre fantasy. Here again we have a situation where simplistic analysis has carried us beyond the realm of technical reality and practical possibility.

The simplistic concepts promulgated around the conjectured neutron bomb of the 1960s are even less applicable to the enhanced radiation warhead of today. This device has been under development for several years in response to an Army requirement for the Lance missile system. Roughly speaking the yield of this warhead is one kiloton, meaning that the blast effect will be one hundred times that of the largest "blockbuster" bomb used in World War II. This fact in itself belies the often heard statement that this device is a weapon which will "save buildings while it kills people." In fact the limiting distances from the explosion at which unprotected people would be killed either by blast or by radiation are very similar. Moreover, the enhancement of the neutron radiation of a 1 KT device produces roughly the same expectance of incapacitating people by neutron radiation (for example an enemy tank crew) as a 10 KT ordinary fission weapon would. Thus the development of the enhanced radiation weapon increases the lethality due to neutron radiation *relative* to that from blast in comparison to more conventional fission weapons, but certainly not to an extent implying a dramatically different situation once nuclear weapons are used at all.

Another point of interest is that the Lance missile system itself at its maximum range of 130 kilometers has a limited accuracy. About half the fired rounds would fall within one-fourth of a mile of the exact target, while the other half is expected to fall outside; any single round can always go considerably beyond this 50 percent radius. *This impact error is not very different from the lethal radius of the radiation effect, or as far as that goes, from the lethal blast radius on unsheltered people.* This fact in itself denies the assertion that under battle conditions this weapon would produce a precisely defined damage radius outside of which everything would remain reasonably intact. Note, too, that under battle conditions, no accuracy can be better than the intelligence information about the enemy positions which guide the firing crew. Since the target against which the neutron bomb is designed is a moving tank, this is not a trivial matter.

Quite apart from these detailed considerations, one should also emphasize that *all* analyses which project low civilian casualties collateral to any significant use of nuclear weapons in Europe are simply wrong. Such studies ignore the streams of refugees which have always accompanied European wars; they assume that cities and their sprawling suburbs are generally removed from where the nuclear explosions are. This is hardly a realistic assumption considering the history of earlier wars, the density of cities, the location of potential tank invasion routes, etc. And then there is fallout. Civilian casualties in any nuclear war in Europe would be vast. For all these reasons, the image of a war fought with "localized" nuclear weapons leaving the host country relatively unscathed is fallacious. It is not surprising that most of our European allies have been less than enthusiastic about being the hosts of neutron bomb deployment.

To summarize, the enhanced radiation warhead is a specialized improvement over ordinary nuclear warheads as an anti-tank weapon. It can kill attacking tank crews with less collateral damage than earlier weapons. But so can other modern anti-tank weapons, not using nuclear weapons at all. Therefore any statement which implies that the development of this weapon marks a quantitative revolution in tactical warfare is false.

It is interesting to contrast this technical situation with the oratory and writing that occurred when this device was identified in the congressional budget.

An interesting fact about the debate is that the critics and supporters of the enhanced radiation warhead tended to reinforce one another in their misstatements about the weapon. The principal assertion was that deployment of this device would lower the "nuclear threshold," i.e., make the initial use of this weapon

33

more acceptable because it would produce less collateral damage, meaning presumably collateral civilian damage, relative to its military effect. This would avoid the "scorched earth" consequences associated with nuclear weapons. Accordingly, so it was argued, engagements with enhanced radiation nuclear weapons would be distinct from those with "ordinary" nuclear weapons and would be so perceived by friend or foe. Therefore *opponents* argued that nuclear war would be easier to initiate, while *proponents* claimed that escalation to large-scale nuclear warfare was less likely to follow. Opponents argued that a decision to initiate use of such a weapon would be easier for a United States President to make, for instance, in case of military threats in Europe. This assertion was denied by President Carter, but in essence the presumed lowered nuclear threshold remained the focus of the debate.

What appeared a virtue to one side—the claim that the enhanced radiation weapon *could* be used without likely nuclear escalation appeared a vice to the opponents. They stated, with great merit, that the *appearance* of lowered risk of escalation would make the weapon more likely to be used and thus the danger of nuclear holocaust would grow. We have seen above that the *technical* merit of either side of this argument is poor, but the very belief in a lowered nuclear threshold adds its own element of danger.

The Soviets jumped into the argument by criticizing the development of the new warhead as being a new round of the arms race and symbolizing lack of restraint of the Carter Administration in pursuing weapons developments. An assembly of European Communist parties, in an unaccustomed show of unity, denounced the new weapon early in August 1977. Paradoxically in November of 1978 Premier Kosygin stated that the Soviet Union had developed such a weapon a long time ago!

As a result of all this oratory (by supposedly knowledgeable and responsible individuals) the perception was created nationally and internationally that the neutron weapon was indeed a major new departure in tactical warfare. In short, what occurred here was that the impression of the nature of the device went greatly beyond its physical reality and this *perception could become a self-fulfilling prophecy.* Happily the Administration, as witnessed by the President's public statements and through the Arms Control Impact Analysis submitted by the National Security Council to the Senate on 13 July 1977, does not seem to share any of the exaggerated description of the importance of the neutron weapon.

The controversy may have a subtle impact on the prospects for agreement on a comprehensive nuclear test ban treaty. One of the factors enhancing the likelihood for attaining a CTBT is the relative saturation or maturity of nuclear weapons technology. Considering the great value of a CTBT in the cause of nonproliferation of nuclear weapons, the opposition by nuclear weapons builders and others on both sides of the curtain may well be blunted by the conviction that in the future developments in non-nuclear weapons technology will be much more important militarily than nuclear achievements. While this conclusion is correct, all the furor surrounding the neutron bomb may contribute to shaking the credibility of this conclusion.

It will be interesting to observe future decisions on the neutron bomb. If physical facts alone were the issues, this matter would probably not have required a major presidential decision or have become the subject of international debate at all. Now, because of the storm of controversy surrounding this one device, the decision has suddenly become a major issue in which such factors as demonstration of resolve, the confidence of our allies, reaction to Soviet criticism, the impression of a lowered nuclear threshold, and the impact on future arms controls created by the controversy itself, will play a substantial role.

Needless to say, while the above discussion documents that the furor around the "neutron bomb" decision is technically ill-founded, the great dilemma remains what doctrine should govern the use of any nuclear weapons in Europe. More than the populations of the United States and the Soviet Union, it is the civilian population of Western Europe that is at risk should the use of nuclear weapons be initiated at all. Even the conventional European wars of the past took millions of civilian lives. How, quite apart from the many considerations in this discussion, could nuclear weapons unleashed *after* a conventional war appears to go badly for one side, lead to less death and devastation?

III

SALT

The foregoing chapters dealt with general considerations regarding the necessity and urgency for progress in arms control, and emphasized measures controlling nuclear weapons. As it happens, the preparation and delivery of this material coincided with the final phases of negotiation of SALT II, which was signed on 18 June 1979. It is therefore of interest to examine that treaty now as it was sent to the Senate for consent to ratification.

The SALT Treaty, Protocol, and Declaration of Principles is a lengthy document, and this is not the place for a detailed analysis. On the contrary, I would like to argue here that overly detailed examination is not essential to reaching sound judgment on the basic merit of SALT II. SALT II is the product of negotiation not only across the bargaining table between representatives of the United States and the U.S.S.R., but also within each country among frequently divergent interests in the civilian and military establishments. As a result, there are in the document certain highly detailed agreements resulting from compromise, and many critics will not find each specific compromise to their liking. However, it is clearly unproductive to deny approval to a treaty which has been negotiated through four administrations and whose history originated in 1967 on grounds that one does not agree with every point.

Appended to this chapter is a document issued by the U.S. State Department that describes in detail the numerical content of SALT II; the text of the full treaty has also been released. As has been pointed out in the previous chapters, caution should be exercised against overinterpreting the quantitative provisions of the treaty, and for this reason I will not join in the popular debate as to whether the numbers favor one side or the other.

There is a great deal of history associated with the numbers, based on unilateral decision-making by the two nations. SALT II does not attempt to redesign the force structure of the two powers along more equitable lines; rather, it applies constraints, where feasible and negotiable, to the existing forces and still arrives at an arms limitation agreement that enhances the security of *both* signatories. SALT is a *process*. The very structure of the agreement is an indicator of the dynamics of negotiation. The *treaty*, running until 1985, represents agreement between the United States and the Soviet Union on numerical limitations, provides for some qualitative constraints, and codifies means to assure verification. The *protocol*, expiring at the end of 1981, represents items on which definitive agreement could not be reached on a long-range basis, but which are restrained for a shorter time, while still preserving freedom of action after expiration of the protocol. The *statement of principles* promises more incisive arms control and touches on those subjects which were not specifically considered, let alone resolved, in SALT I and II. A separate exchange of statements between the Soviet President and President Carter deals with controls on the Soviet "Backfire" medium-size bomber.

B. THE CONTENT OF SALT II

1. *The Treaty*

Numerically the treaty obeys the mandate imposed by the amendment enacted by the U.S. Senate as part of the ratification process of SALT I, implying that the total number of "strategic nuclear delivery vehicles" (SNDVs) of the two parties shall be equal. By the term "SNDV" we mean the totality of intercontinental missile launchers based either on land or sea, plus the number of strategic carriers of bombs or missiles. Starting from this basic number (2,250 by 1982) there are then various subcategories which are controlled separately. First the sum of the launchers for MIRVed missiles and carriers of cruise missiles is constrained; then the total number of launchers for MIRVed missiles is limited; and finally the maximum number of land-based MIRVed ICBM launchers is specified. To conform to these numerical ceilings the Soviet Union will have to destroy about 250 launcher systems now operational, while the United States can proceed as now planned without affecting its systems now in operation.

In addition to these basic quantitative constraints there are more specific quantitative limitations, some of which are of great importance. Most significant is the so-called "fractionation limit" through which the number of MIRVs carried by each ICBM and SLBM (submarine-launched ballistic missile) is limited to the maximum number tested and deployed at the time of the treaty. For instance without the fractionation limit the largest of Soviet missiles, the SS-18, could carry perhaps thirty warheads, while SALT II will freeze that number at ten. The combination of that constraint with the previous ones means that there is an absolute limit on the number of missile-borne nuclear weapons which threaten the United States. Conversely the average number of cruise missiles carried on aircraft is restricted (but not their range). Such ALCMs (air-launched cruise missiles) are now under active development and testing by the United States.

Note that SALT II limits launchers and not missiles. This means in principle that either party could produce large quantities of missiles and stockpile them to permit the reloading of existing launchers after the first set of missiles had been dispatched. SALT II limits the stockpiling of such possible reserve missiles to sites far away from the launchers, so that should either side contemplate such a tactic, there would be a very substantial time delay before such reloading could be effective. Formally such stockpiling leading to a delayed reload capability would not be a violation of the treaty. However, considering the time delay before reloading, such a step would be expensive and militarily not very effective. In addition, such stockpiling, were it to reach significant quantities, could hardly escape detection since substantial production and support activities would be required. This general set of circumstances should be remembered by those critics who cite reload capability as a substantial reason why the choice of limiting launchers rather than missiles in SALT II was an unwise decision.

The qualitative restrictions of the SALT II Treaty are less impressive. For land-based missiles the treaty permits one "new system," which accommodates the MX missile now under development in the United States, and on the Soviet side one (possibly single warhead) follow-on system to one of their older ICBMs. The older systems may be modernized to a limited extent consistent with leaving certain sizes and weights of measurable quantities unchanged. Note that this set of restrictions, although permitting only one totally new ICBM for each side, still permits continuous upgrading of such characteristics as missile accuracy, reliability, and warhead explosive power, all of which contribute to their threat. Note also that modernization or the introduction of totally new systems of submarine launched weapons or of strategic aircraft are not limited.

2. The Protocol

The protocol has two essential provisions: first, it forbids flight testing and deployment, but not development, of launchers for mobile ICBMs; and second, it forbids deployment, but not research, development, and testing, of ground-launched and sea-launched cruise missiles of range longer than six hundred kilometers. Air-launched cruise missiles are not restricted in the protocol. Some comments on these provisions are in order.

Neither the United States nor the Soviet Union currently has operational mobile land-based ICBMs deployed. The Soviets had developed an off-road mobile system, the SS-16. However, SALT II explicitly forbids the SS-16 and evidence is persuasive that the system has been dismounted and production discontinued. Discussions about United States mobile systems have been going on for over a decade, and systems which can be described as "mobile" are being developed as possible modes of basing the MX missile now under development. It is impossible for any U.S. mobile system to reach the test phase, let alone the deployment phase, before expiration of the protocol. Therefore the protocol, unless its terms are extended, will not constrain U.S. programs in any way in respect to mobile missiles. Long-range ground-based and sea-launched cruise missiles are under current development in the United States, and they are designed to play a possible role in the defense of Western Europe. For reasons touched on in the previous chapter, it is, however, far from clear whether and where an acceptable deployment pattern and doctrine for use of these weapons in Western Europe can be established. Again, in this respect the protocol provisions are drawn up in such a way that U.S. programs would only be affected if the terms of the protocol were extended. The United States has made absolutely sure that the negotiating record of SALT be clear that the United States preserves its total freedom of action after expiration of the protocol, and it is possible that during the Senate debate a resolution will be generated that any extension of the protocol must meet with Senate approval similar to that accorded a full treaty. Thus the United States has retained its flexibility in respect to deployment plans for mobile ballistic missiles and cruise missiles of all kinds.

Originally the Soviets insisted, in connection with the cruise missile, that the parties should be forbidden to transfer hardware or technology relating to items controlled by the treaty to third parties. The United States objected to this initiative, since it would clearly inhibit military cooperation between the United States and it NATO allies. The matter was settled by a "non-circumvention clause" under which the parties are enjoined from transferring materials and technology so as to circumvent the provisions of the treaty, but are permitted to make such transfers in all other circumstances. While this formulation may leave some margin for interpretation, it definitely does not prevent the United States from cooperating with NATO in cruise missile technology, should that be decided upon.

3. The Exchange of Statements on Backfire

The exchange of statements between heads of state has the same legal standing as the treaty and protocol in that violation of the statements would have the same consequences as that of the other documents. The statement restricts production rates and upgrading related to the Backfire bomber to assure the United States that it is not deployed as an intercontinental strategic weapons system. Technically, the Backfire could have such a mission if suitably based and supported; its range can be adequate for such a purpose. However, U.S. designers and analysts agree that the Backfire is a poorly designed vehicle for strategic purposes; in fact we understand quite well many of the uses for European warfare and anti-ship missions for which Backfire is being deployed.

C. VERIFICATION

1. *Standards*

In addition to providing quantitative limits and qualitative constraints SALT provides for aids to facilitate verification of the agreement. The term "verification," of course, means the provision of assurance that the parties obey the agreement. There can be and is a wide spectrum of opinion on how to assure that verification will be "adequate." As in respect to civil law enforcement, it would be unreasonable to demand that a law should not be passed unless the citizens can be assured that *any* transgression of that law can be brought to justice. At the other extreme, it would also be unreasonable to pass a law if no significant means were provided to assure compliance. Clearly the standards of verification of a strategic arms limitation treaty must bear some relationship to the importance of the potential transgression to be policed. In general, "adequate verification" means that any violation of the terms of the treaty or protocol, while they are in force, should be "verifiable" if such transgression affects significantly the military strategic relationship between the signatories.

Note that the foregoing discussion ignores the political aspects but relates to the adequacy of verification for strictly military purposes. Some argue that unless we can assure the American people that *any* violation can be detected by the United States there would be residual doubt about the good faith of the Soviet Union in signing SALT. One can argue conversely as to why the Soviet Union should carry out small violations if they would have little significant military importance but would still involve some risk of detection—there is always some such risk of possible leaks through U.S. informers, Soviet defectors, etc. More important, this is a bridge which we have already crossed. The United States has signed with the Soviet Union and other parties such treaties as the treaty forbidding biological warfare, the treaty limiting weapons of mass destruction in outer space, etc. These treaties are not verifiable in total detail. For instance, biological weapons could be hidden rather easily. Yet it has been recognized by all parties that biological weapons are not apt to be decisive, and in many cases not even a usable means of warfare, while their danger to humanity is substantial. Thus the incomplete verifiability of the treaty forbidding biological weapons is compensated by the limited military importance of such weapons.

None of this discussion implies that verification of SALT II is marginal; on the contrary, I would conclude that it is quite substantial and insensitive to variations in circumstances affecting intelligence collection. It is unfortunate that there continues to be a debate regarding verifiability of SALT measured against a standard requiring detectability of *any* violation.

2. Means of Verification

Verification is based on all of the means that each country possesses for gathering intelligence about the other country's activities. Such collectors include reconnaissance satellites that are sensitive to a variety of emissions from military systems or production facilities of the other side. In fact, it is well for critics of technology to remember that the advent of surveillance satellites has in a real sense made our world more open. In addition, installations either at sea or on land outside the boundaries of the other side monitor militarily related activities, and there can also be clandestine observation of activities of interest. The latter type of activity is in no way legitimized by SALT, which, however, explicitly protects the right to collect intelligence on the other side's activities by "national technical means." Each country's ability to verify compliance with SALT is based on the *sum* of its intelligence collection assets, and it is a natural feature of such assets that they are continuously changing. On the technical side, progressive improvements are made in the quality and quantity of information which can be gathered. The sum of the means of observation can go up or down, depending on several factors: the total effort and money each country is willing to put into them, the success of measures to conceal military activities, and the access that countries not directly participating in the treaty are willing to give to stations or overflights collecting intelligence. This general pattern should be kept in mind when one reacts to such events as the recent loss of Iranian tracking stations. Clearly the denial by the Iranians of continued U.S.

operation of such stations has decreased U.S. monitoring capability, but these stations are only a part of a very large number of diverse systems. It does not take much insight to recognize that verification of the basic numerical provisions of SALT II—that is, the counting of launchers, submarines, and aircraft—is not dependent on the type of ground-station represented by the Iranian installation, but depends on surveillance from above. In contrast, some of the specific measurements which must be made to evaluate compliance with the dimensional limits implied by the regulations on permitted modernization of existing missiles depend on information from many sources. Any physical measurements, and measurements related to verification are no exception, have a certain probable error, and this probable error naturally will increase as tools for conducting such measurements are denied. Without going into detail, precision of such measurements is not critical in determining whether potential violations of SALT would significantly affect the military balance, and therefore the degree of precision would not relate to the question as to whether verification is "adequate." Therefore, in accordance with the standards and available U.S. collection systems discussed, I would conclude that SALT II verification is fully adequate.

SALT II continues a number of institutional and procedural arrangements codified in SALT I for *cooperation* in respect to verification, and adds some additional provisions.

SALT II continues the so-called *nonconcealment* provisions. This means that both sides are prevented from concealing their customary procedures of deploying missiles, launching submarines, etc., by deceptive practices such as covers, camouflage, etc. Again this is a provision that increases confidence in compliance with the treaty. Should such a nonconcealment provision in itself be violated, this would clearly be evident. A cooperative verification measure similar to nonconcealment is the SALT II provision that limits the permitted degree of *encryption* (i.e., coding) of missile test telemetry data. The degree of permitted encryption is defined so as not to "impede verification of compliance with the provisions of the treaty." Let me explain: a substantial contribution to the ability of the United States to understand the nature and performance of Soviet missiles stems from the interception of telemetry of Soviet missile tests, i.e., the signals sent to ground observers by instruments carried on board a test flight. This contribution to verification could be denied by either party through encryption of the information. The specific agreement on this subject had to meet the U.S. desire for the maintenance of this very useful means of verification, while meeting the Soviet pressure to keep secret what was not explicitly controlled by SALT II.

The existing Standing Consultative Commission (SCC) is continued. This is a body before which evidence of suspicious events and alleged violations of the treaty provisions can be brought. The commission encompasses representatives from both parties and meets in privacy. This body has been remarkably effective as part of SALT I—charges of allegedly ambiguous events have been brought before the SCC by *both* parties and have been discussed in remarkable detail. *It is interesting to note that no evidence of deliberate cheating by either party has been uncovered.* Both parties have engaged in inadvertent or minor transgressions which have been corrected after referral to the SCC. This record should be considered by the critics of verifiability of SALT II. Most important is the fact that the SCC has been a forum of discussion between U.S. and Soviet representatives of sensitive military subjects whose discussion would have been unthinkable only a few years ago.

D. EVALUATION OF SALT

1. General Assessment

There should be little question whether the SALT I and II treaties enhance United States and world security. SALT I has reduced missile defenses to what are militarily insignificant quantities and has thus assured each side that their ballistic missile reentry warheads, if successfully launched, will penetrate. SALT has opened up and maintained a dialogue between the United States and the Soviet Union on subjects which had been heretofore undiscussable. SALT has codified verification processes in such a way as to greatly ease the assured access by the U.S. to knowledge of Soviet strategic weapons. SALT II places quantitative ceilings and limited qualitative constraints on various categories of long-range nuclear weapons. As a result each side, when preparing intelligence projections for the distant future, is significantly limited in the upward excursions of such projections. Thus the future is less uncertain. Moreover, some actual destruction of older weapons systems by the Soviets will take place as a result of SALT, and one can argue persuasively, since today the Soviets have more momentum in weapons buildup than the United States, that the SALT ceilings have worked out to a net U.S. advantage. SALT has initiated a *process* which beams a ray of hope that the arms race between the United States and the U.S.S.R. may avoid the ultimate disaster.

Yet despite all these positive achievements of SALT I and II, one has to conclude that the enactment of these treaties has only a relatively small technical impact on the evolution of the strategic arms race between the United States and the Soviet Union. If one projects the strategic future that would accrue had there been no SALT treaties, and compares it with the future that we can foresee with SALT enacted, then numbers differ but little, *although SALT II definitely reduces the burden of nuclear weaponry*. One has to agree that the evolution of military technology which took place during the process of negotiating the SALT treaties has been more rapid than the limitations which enactment of the SALT treaties imposes. Thus on technical grounds alone, SALT has done relatively little to reduce the risks this nation or the Soviet Union might face from possible nuclear war. Therefore while on broader grounds I would conclude that SALT should be strongly supported, I see little solely technical reason for great enthusiasm in praising the achievements of SALT II.

Yet despite the limited technical value of SALT II, it has become a big political issue. In fact, the SALT debate encompasses the prospects for improvements or degeneration of U.S./Soviet relations and most phases of past and future military decisions and policies of the United States.

Clearly we have here again an example where the political impact of a military issue, in this case a specific step in arms control, has outrun the technical realities. Why has this happened? One clear reason is that the SALT negotiating process has in itself tended to inflate in the public mind the importance of the issues under negotiation with the Soviets. The increasing mistrust of secret diplomacy, accentuated by Watergate, that has accumulated in recent times has resulted in de facto open reporting of each issue as it arises in negotiation. As a result, even small numerical gaps in the positions of the negotiating parties have been given exaggerated importance. Even disagreements about the time of commencement of the treaty obligations became major issues. Thus the negotiating process itself has given an unwarranted importance to the *numerology* relating to the strategic arms race. In contrast, the "new openness" of the negotiations has done little to provide public insight into the overriding issues, in particular the real nature of nuclear war and the dangers and burdens of the growing nuclear weapons stockpiles.

Thus the SALT debate goes much beyond its actual content. A large part of the dialogue is centered around issues that are hardly related to the terms of SALT at all. There are first the deeply troublesome issues raised by the increasing military effort of the Soviet Union. Then there are side issues such as the following: Can one trust the Russians? Does signature of SALT signal approval of Soviet conduct or ideology? How can we agree to a SALT treaty negotiated by the same administration that gave up the B-1 bomber and did not go forward with the neutron bomb? Aren't we disarming enough already?

None of these questions is a relevant criticism of SALT. As discussed in previous chapters, it is the very essence of effective arms control that mutual trust is not a precondition. Verification procedures must be sufficiently reliable so that opportunities for unmonitored evasion by the U.S.S.R. involve acceptable risks to the United States and little incentive to the Soviets. Signing a SALT agreement is not a reward for good conduct on the part of the Soviet Union, nor does it imply approval of decisions made by this or past administrations of various actions in weapons procurement or military policy. *The merit of SALT must be judged on the basis of whether U.S. security and world security would be greater or less with SALT—and by that test the answer is clearly positive.*

In this broad context, security depends not only on minimizing the risk of military conflict and improving the chance for a favorable outcome of a possible war, but also upon the political situation, and in particular on the relations between the United States and the Soviet Union. Our economic condition and the confidence of our allies are major security issues. All these factors are affected by SALT, and enactment of SALT II should improve security in terms of these relationships. However, these predictable political linkages will be affected by how in the public debate we deal with those broader security issues. In short, we have again created a situation where the political perception of an arms control process is affected by arguments that are irrelevent on strictly technical grounds, but where these political perceptions will ultimately affect the achievements of that agreement.

2. *Criticisms of SALT II*

In this chapter we have outlined SALT as a process and the contents of the SALT II Treaty. Ratification is currently in doubt. It therefore seems appropriate to discuss the arguments that are frequently heard against ratification. It is unfortunate that so much of the debate swirling around ratification tends not to deal with the substance of SALT II itself, but serves rather as an expression of discontent with military decisions of the current or past administrations, with the status of military policy, or just plain dissatisfaction with the fact that the United States, which contains less than 6 percent of the world's population, can no longer command as controlling a position in the world as it did decades ago.

Criticism of SALT tends to fall into two general categories: that originating from the "Hawks," that is, from those who feel that U.S. security might be endangered by enactment of SALT II; and from the "Doves," who feel that SALT II accomplishes too little arms control at too large a political or financial cost. Most criticisms from the "Hawk" side flow from the critics' analysis of the Soviet military buildup, and SALT's failure to have prevented that growth. SALT is thus held responsible by some for proclaimed inferiorities in the U.S. strategic military posture. Although the overall U.S. strategic position remains strong, there are many selected areas where the relative U.S. position is becoming weaker. The emerging SALT debate provides a convenient platform for voicing concern about any defense issue. However, it is simply wrong to hold SALT responsible for any of the claimed deficiencies.

The assertion that the United States is in a strategically inferior position has little basis. Those who proclaim an emerging inferiority tend to quote selected indices of measuring the relative power of the two nations in which the Soviet Union is ahead, in particular the throw-weight of land-based missiles, the number of air-defense systems, the expenditures on civilian defense, etc. In particular, emphasis is placed on the emerging problem of Minuteman vulnerability based on the undisputed fact that technically by the early 1980s an attack by Soviet ICBMs against the U.S. Minuteman force could destroy well over 90 percent of those missiles. As has been discussed extensively in the previous chapters, and as we will discuss shortly in more detail in reference to Minuteman, such selective quotations are greatly misleading. It is equally possible and equally meaningless to quote selected indices that demonstrate U.S. superiority. For instance, the United States leads in the number of missile warheads, in the number of strategic airplanes, in the technology of air-launched and other cruise missiles, in missile accuracy, etc., etc. Again, as has been discussed in previous chapters, such simple quantitative indices have very little relationship to predicting the outcome of an actual potential conflict.

There are many other criteria that are much more difficult to quantify, such as geographical differences, the strength of alliances, the number and power of unfriendly neighbors, etc. Above all, nuclear war is so strongly dependent on the human element—the decision-making process and the behavior of populations and governments under stress—that the simplistic measures of relative power are grossly misleading. However, irrespective of the details of these numbers, and irrespective of whether SALT II enters into force, for at least a decade ahead each country faces devastating retaliation should it attack the other first with nuclear weapons. At the risk of redundancy let me emphasize again that if nuclear war is initiated for any purpose, under any strategy, by any country, then the populations of both the Soviet Union and the United States are in the gravest danger.

A criticism arising from concern about U.S. strategic strength is that SALT will give us a "false sense of security" and could thereby make it much more difficult in the future to provide for those measures which are necessary for defending the United States and its interests. Note that such criticism rarely, if ever, addresses itself to the provisions of SALT II itself. The reason is clear: none of the programs which advocate higher defense spending and more aggressive military policies for the United States would be constrained by SALT II. For instance, no such initiatives as expanded civil defense, further acceleration in cruise missile development, the development, testing, and deployment of MX mobile missiles, reactivating the B-1 program, etc., are inhibited by the terms of SALT. Therefore the criticism so often voiced that SALT will interfere directly with a strong defense refers to a psychological interference rather than any inhibition by the provisions of the treaty. The sad commentary on such criticism is that it could apply to any arms control agreement. It essentially perpetuates the view that negotiated agreement with a potential adversary is an expression of weakness.

It is illuminating to note that the Hawkish criticism that SALT will generate a false sense of security and thereby impede needed defense procurements is directly paired with the criticism made by "Doves" that ratification of SALT II will exact too high a price in terms of increased defense spending. The basis for this concern is that ratification of SALT as a practical political matter demands consensus by a wide segment of America concerned with security affairs. Specifically, the necessary two-thirds majority in the Senate for ratification will be difficult to secure if there is explicit opposition to the treaty by military representatives, in particular the Joint Chiefs of Staff. Thus the Joint Chiefs of Staff are in a strong bargaining position within the government to exact guarantees for increased support of military weapons systems in exchange for their support of the treaty. Although this argument enters into the ratification debate at various levels of subtlety, it has a certain degree of reality.

Although both of the above arguments have some merit, it is very difficult for me to believe that the existence of a SALT treaty would militate against the United States acting in its own best interest. Naturally, there always has been and always will be debate about national priorities in allocating resources—guns versus butter—but SALT is only a very minor factor in such a debate.

Now let us turn from the general to the specific criticisms.

a. Minuteman Vulnerability. It has been recognized ever since the United States decided to place fixed silos in the fields of North Dakota and other states that as the Soviets would deploy similar weapons carrying MIRVs of high accuracy, the safety of these silos could become endangered. The statement that SALT II has failed to eliminate the vulnerability of Minuteman is correct. Yet it is hardly proper to fault SALT II because it did not attain a goal it was not designed to reach. Moreover, SALT II does not limit the choice of U.S. remedial action in response to the Minuteman problem. In fact, since SALT II limits the number of warheads that the Soviets may deploy, it would make the design of countermeasures more tractable.

Minuteman vulnerability is just one of the many elements in the U.S./U.S.S.R. strategic relationship which must be considered in evaluating the standing of the two nations, but it is hardly a controlling one. Although by the early 1980s the Soviets could indeed attack successfully an overwhelming fraction of the Minuteman force, they would do so only at the risk of retaliation by our surviving sea-launched and airborne strategic nuclear forces, which carry roughly 75 percent of the total U.S. retaliatory power. In contrast, while the United States in the same epoch could not successfully wipe out an overwhelming fraction of the U.S.S.R. land-based force, it could destroy roughly one-half of that force in a preemptive strike. Since the U.S.S.R. has chosen to incorporate almost 80 percent of its total retaliatory power in its land-based ICBMs, such an attack would reduce Soviet total residual forces by a larger fraction than an attack against the U.S. ICBMs by the U.S.S.R. In short, the vulnerability of the land-based ICBMs which had been predicted for well over a decade poses a much graver problem in the long run to the Soviet Union than it does to the United States. Therefore, the criticism that SALT II has not succeeded in eliminating the problem of Minuteman vulnerability is unfair when voiced in a one-sided way. Yet it is true that, SALT or no SALT, the increasing vulnerability of the land-based ICBM forces has added an element of instability to the strategic relationship between the two superpowers. If one broadly interprets one of the purposes of arms control as decreasing the risk of war by achieving greater stability, then this increasing vulnerability is a factor counteracting this goal of arms control, and future agreements must address this problem.

b. The B-1 Cancellation. The decision by President Carter to cancel production of the B-1 bomber is frequently cited as an act of unilateral disarmament related to SALT. The argument is made that the President should not have taken this step without getting a reciprocal concession from the Soviets. Yet by substituting an accelerated air-launched cruise missile (ALCM) program for the B-1, the President has actually greatly complicated the task of the arms controller: from the SALT point of view the B-1 is just another strategic airplane which, under the counting rules of SALT, would enter into the SALT equation in the same way as the older B-52s. The presidential decision was based entirely on projected costs versus military effectiveness. Although some disagree with the President's conclusion that he could buy more defense at lesser cost by canceling the B-1 and accelerating the cruise missile program, the fact is that this was surely not a concession to the Soviets, nor, as far as that goes, did it serve the interests of arms control.

c. The Future of the Protocol. Some maintain that the provisions of the protocol will automatically be extended after the protocol expires in 1981, and the treaty will likewise continue, irrespective of merit. Yet the negotiating record is replete with U.S. statements asserting freedom of action after termination of the protocol. Indeed, should the experience with SALT II, once enacted, be satisfactory, then the burden of opposing its extension will become heavier. On the other hand, if arguments based on a more negative SALT experience and on an increasing threat from the opponent become more persuasive, then there should be little difficulty in resisting pressures for extension. Either way it seems unjustifiable to oppose enactment of the protocol by maintaining that this country would be unable to make wise decisions in its own interest several years hence.

The question of the future of the protocol is principally an issue relating to European security. It is therefore worth noting that the political leaders of all West European countries have strongly endorsed SALT II.

d. Backfire Should Be Included in the Strategic Total in the Treaty. Backfire is a new Soviet bomber considerably smaller than the U.S. strategic B-52, but larger than the Europe-based F-111; both of the U.S. bombers can carry nuclear weapons to the U.S.S.R. Technically the Backfire can carry out intercontinental missions from the U.S.S.R. to most of the U.S. territory, but there is full agreement that it is poorly designed for such a purpose. The criticism is then: Why were the agreed-upon restrictions on Backfire codified in a separate exchange of statements rather than as part of the SALT II Treaty? Why is Backfire not included in the total count of strategic delivery vehicles?

The answer is based on the long history of SALT as it relates to weapons in the European theater. At the inception of SALT, the Soviets took the position that since SALT deals with strategic weapons, all weapons of one party which threaten the homeland of the other should be considered strategic and be included in SALT. Under this definition the so-called "forward based systems" (FBS) of the United States, such as the F-111 bombers and the F-4 fighters which are based in Europe and could deliver nuclear weapons to the western U.S.S.R., are strategic, while the large SS-4 and SS-5 intermediate range ballistic missiles, among others, which threaten Western Europe but not the United States, would not be included. The United States objected to this interpretation of "strategic," pointing out that inclusion of FBS would introduce the entire question of European security. The disagreement on FBS systems was the reason why in SALT I a *treaty* on offensive nuclear arms was not agreed upon, and only an *interim agreement* dealing with offensive weapons, excluding consideration of aircraft, was reached. In SALT II the Soviets, *as a concession to the United States,* agreed to drop FBS altogether, but emphasized that once larger reductions were to be considered in the future the FBS matter would reemerge. The Backfire is clearly designed for European warfare and anti-submarine purposes, although its range is marginally intercontinental. Therefore the United States could not force the Soviets during negotiation to incorporate the agreed-upon restriction on Backfire into the treaty without reopening the whole FBS issue. The separate, legally binding exchange of statements was the compromise solution.

3. The Future of SALT

The statement of principles of SALT II commits the United States and the Soviet Union to negotiate a SALT III agreement, and all indications are that once ratification has been achieved, or even before, negotiations will quickly resume. Some general remarks on future directions may be helpful.

The foregoing paragraphs relating to problems of Backfire and the protocol are of only indirect intercontinental strategic significance, and mainly concern Western Europe. In general the question of limiting the evolution of the threat of nuclear warfare in Europe is casting an increasing shadow over the SALT negotiations. Many nuclear weapons systems which relate to Western Europe emerged during the long period between 1967, when the SALT process was initiated, and today. For instance, longer range cruise missiles and the Backfire bomber were complications whose existence did not intrude upon the early phases of the negotiations. Both of these systems have the common feature that under certain circumstances their role could be considered either strategic or tactical, that is, for use in the European theater. This pattern constitutes a problem that future SALT negotiations, should the process continue, will have to face. The boundary line between tactical and strategic systems will continue to be eroded by technology. The so-called "gray area systems," which could have roles in either strategic or tactical warfare, will increase in number. With the emergence of gray area systems it will become progressively more difficult to restrict SALT to a purely bilateral forum. The reason why a negotiation involving only the United States and the Soviet Union appeared promising for curbing the nuclear arms race is that the two superpowers possess over 99 percent of the world's nuclear weapons, and the relations between each superpower and third parties would not be substantially affected by limitations on these nuclear weapons. Yet, owing to both the evolution of gray area systems and the emergence of China as a threat to the Soviet Union, a bilateral SALT process appears to have become a perishable commodity. Clearly in SALT III, should it proceed, consultation with the European allies must be intensified, although it would be impractical to involve NATO and Warsaw Pact countries as direct parties in the negotiation.

The above remark is just one example in support of the conclusion that *the pace of military technology has outstripped the rate of progress of arms control.* Although SALT II will place U.S. security in a much better position than it would be should ratification fail, the fact remains that the SALT process must accomplish more and move faster if in the long run it is to reverse the buildup of nuclear armament, both in numbers and performance.

The visible agenda for SALT III indicated by the unfinished business of the protocol and the terms of the statement of principles is hardly adequate in itself to offer much optimism that the present dynamics of U.S./Soviet negotiations will achieve the necessary deeper cuts at a sufficient rate. The likely inclusion of gray area systems is a further complication. Yet a rising awareness of the overriding need for arms limitations may force the necessary acceleration of real arms control through modification of the SALT process. Speedy ratification of SALT II is an essential step.

The process leading from the first meeting in 1967 between President Johnson and Premier Kosygin at Glassboro, New Jersey, which initiated SALT has been a long one. We have gone through several administrations, through a treaty and interim agreement and protocol, and now a further treaty and protocol are on the way. During that time there has been increasing public exposure of each SALT negotiating step under continually changing circumstances.

The technical community has a continuing major responsibility to inform the general public and political leaders about the real nature and enormous risks of the nuclear tools of war. The SALT process is the *only* path now in view which extends any hope that the truly insane accumulation of weapons, larger than can serve any justifiable military purpose, can be limited and reversed. To reach this goal we must not permit this awesome physical threat to be concealed under the rhetoric and symbolism that is used in the political discourse. If this occurs, humanity loses its ability to answer the fateful question: When is there enough?

A Special Report

SALT II
Basic Guide

United States Department of State
Bureau of Public Affairs

Washington, D.C.

Background

The Strategic Arms Limitation Talks (SALT) had its genesis during the Johnson Administration. The United States approached the Soviet Union in 1967 on the possibility of Strategic Arms Limitation Talks with the expressed objective of limiting anti-ballistic missile systems. The Soviet Union agreed that such limitations could be in our mutual interest and suggested that the sides should also examine the possibility of limiting offensive systems as well. However, the Soviet invasion of Czechoslovakia in August of 1968 delayed the start of these negotiations.

When the Nixon Administration took office, the idea of initiating strategic arms limitation talks immediately came up again. The Soviet Union reaffirmed its interest and willingness to commence such negotiations, and in November of 1969 the SALT negotiations formally began.

The first phase of SALT—which became known as SALT I—culminated in 1972 with the completion and ratification of two agreements. The first agreement—the ABM Treaty—restricted the deployment of antiballistic missile systems by the United States and the Soviet Union to equal and very low levels. The second agreement—the Interim Agreement on Strategic Offensive Arms—froze the number of offensive strategic ballistic missile launchers at the number then deployed or under construction by each country. The ABM Treaty was of unlimited duration, while the Interim Agreement was to last for a period of five years.

Building upon the foundation laid by SALT I, the United States and the Soviet Union began a subsequent series of negotiations—SALT II—in November of 1972. The objective of these negotiations was to replace the Interim Agreement with a long-term, comprehensive and balanced agreement limiting strategic offensive weapons.

Throughout the past six years, three American Presidents have continued these negotiations. Their common objective has been to reduce the danger of nuclear war by bringing under control a potentially dangerous strategic arms competition.

A major breakthrough for the SALT II negotiations occurred at the Vladivostok meeting in November 1974, between President Gerald Ford and General Secretary Leonid Brezhnev. At this meeting the two sides agreed to a number of the basic elements for the SALT II agreement, including an equal overall limit on the offensive strategic forces of both nations.

The SALT II Agreement

The SALT II agreement consists of three basic parts: a treaty to last until the end of 1985; a shorter term protocol that will expire on December 31, 1981; and a joint statement of principles and basic guidelines for subsequent negotiations. In addition, SALT II includes a commitment by the Soviet Union on the issue of the Soviet Backfire bomber; an agreed memorandum listing the numbers of strategic weapons deployed by each side according to various categories; and a lengthy set of agreed statements and common understandings which set forth interpretations with respect to many of the provisions of SALT II.

The provisions of the treaty fall into three major categories: quantitative limits, qualitative limits, and verification measures.

Quantitative Limits

The treaty restricts the United States and the Soviet Union to an equal, overall total of strategic nuclear delivery vehicles. The equality of this limitation redresses an imbalance in favor of the USSR that has existed since prior to the signing of the SALT I agreements. The units to be included under this ceiling are land-based intercontinental ballistic missile (ICBM) launchers, submarine-launched ballistic missile (SLBM) launchers, heavy bombers, and air-to-surface ballistic missiles (ASBM's) with ranges over 600 km. Within this agreed ceiling, a number of subceilings have been placed on specific types of nuclear systems. The limits are as follows:

The initial ceiling for all ICBM launchers, SLBM launchers, heavy bombers, and ASBM's is 2,400. This ceiling will be reduced to 2,250 by December 31, 1981. Under these limits, the Soviet Union, now at a level of about 2,520, will be required to remove about 270 strategic nuclear delivery vehicles from its weapons inventory, while the United States, now at a level of about 2,060 operational systems, will be allowed to augment its strategic forces slightly under the terms of the overall ceiling. This limitation will also prevent the Soviet Union from further expanding its current strategic forces to a level of as much as 3,000 delivery systems that could be deployed by the end of 1985.

A subceiling of 1,320 applies to the total number of launchers of strategic ballistic missiles equipped with multiple independently-targetable re-entry vehicles (MIRV's) plus heavy bombers equipped with cruise missiles with ranges over 600 km.

An additional subceiling of 1,200 applies to the total number of launchers of MIRV'ed ballistic missiles. The USSR could deploy several hundred MIRV'ed missile launchers in excess of this total in the absence of a SALT II agreement.

The final subceiling restricts each nation to the deployment of no more than 820 MIRV'ed ICBM launchers. This restriction is especially important because it will limit the deployment of MIRV'ed systems by the USSR and because MIRV'ed ICBM's are potentially the most destabilizing type of strategic nuclear delivery vehicle.

The construction of additional fixed ICBM launchers is banned by the SALT II treaty, and neither nation is permitted to increase the number of its fixed launchers for heavy ICBM's—defined as ICBM's with a launch-weight (weight of the total missile) or throw-weight (weight of the useful payload of the missile) greater than that of the Soviet SS-19 missile. The Soviet Union is the only nation which has deployed modern, large ballistic missiles of this type.

Allotment of Strategic Nuclear Delivery Vehicles

Total Delivery Systems

Each country is limited initially to 2400 strategic nuclear delivery vehicles of all types combined—i.e., land-based intercontinental ballistic missile (ICBM) launchers, submarine-launched ballistic missile (SLBM) launchers, air-to-surface ballistic missiles (ASBM's) capable of a range in excess of 600 kilometers, and heavy bombers. In 1981, the initial 2400 total will be reduced to 2250. Within this overall ceiling there will be sub-limits imposed equally on both sides.

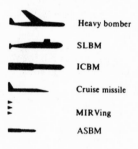

Heavy bomber

SLBM

ICBM

Cruise missile

MIRVing

ASBM

1982 Total

Combined strategic nuclear delivery vehicles
of all types: 2250

2250

Sublimit 1

Of the 2250, neither side is permitted more than
a combined total of 1320 of the following types:
1) Launchers of MIRVed ICBM's 2) Launchers
of MIRVed SLBM's 3) heavy bombers
equipped for long-range cruise missiles and 4)
MIRVed ASBM's.

1320

Sublimit 2

Of the 1320, neither side is permitted more
than a combined total of 1200 1) Launchers
of MIRVed ICBM's 2) Launchers of MIRVed
SLBM's, and 3) MIRVed ASBM's.

1200

Sublimit 3

Of the 1200, neither side is permitted more than
820 Launchers of MIRVed ICBM's.

820

Qualitative Limits

The treaty places a number of qualitative restrictions on the development and deployment of new types of nuclear weapons. These limitations include:

The number of warheads on currently existing types of ICBM's is frozen at existing levels, i.e., at the maximum number tested on each particular type of ICBM, as a means of slowing the expansion in the number of nuclear warheads. As a consequence, the Soviets will be permitted a maximum of 10 warheads on their heavy missiles—whereas without this limit, they might easily deploy 20 or 30 warheads on a modification of the SS-18.

SLBM's will be limited to no more than 14 warheads, the maximum number that has been tested by either side to date.

The throw-weight and total-missile weight of light ICBM's, SLBM's, and ASBM's cannot exceed that of the Soviet SS-19; similar limits apply to increasing the throw-weight and launch-weight of heavy ICBM's beyond those of the SS-18. This will limit the further growth in the payload delivery capability of missiles.

Each side will be permitted to test and deploy only one new type of ICBM for the duration of the treaty. This exception gives the United States the right to proceed with the M-X missile. In permitting the Soviets only one new type of ICBM, this provision will inhibit the Soviets in their past practice of deploying three or four completely new types of ICBM's, with substantially different and improved characteristics, with each new generation of ICBM's.

The permitted new type of ICBM must be a light ICBM (i.e., its throw-weight cannot exceed that of the SS-19), and it cannot have more than 10 warheads. The Soviet Union may choose to use its exemption to deploy a single warhead missile, or it may deploy a new MIRV'ed missile to replace the SS-17 and SS-19. The M-X missile will probably carry the maximum permitted number of 10 warheads and will have three times the throw-weight of the Minuteman.

The average number of long-range (i.e., over 600 km) cruise missiles that can be deployed by either nation aboard its airplanes equipped for such missiles can be no greater than 28. The maximum number of longrange cruise missiles that can be deployed on existing heavy bombers, such as the B-52, is limited to 20. Any aircraft that is equipped with longrange cruise missiles is counted as an ALCM-carrying heavy bomber and is included in the SALT II numerical aggregates.

Verification Measures

To insure that the United States will be able by its own means to verify Soviet compliance with the terms of SALT II, the agreement contains a number of provisions designed to enhance the ability of the United States to police Soviet conduct with regard to weapons included in the agreement.

The agreement prohibits any deliberate concealment activities which impede verification of compliance with the provisions of the agreement. A clarification to this provision notes that any telemetry encryption (that is, the encoding of missile and aircraft test data) which impedes verification is banned.

The agreement also forbids any interference by one nation with the operation of the intelligence collection systems (referred to in the treaty as "national technical means" or "NTM") belonging to the other nation and used to verify compliance with the provisions of the agreement.

Since it is difficult to distinguish between MIRV'ed and non-MIRV'ed types of missiles once they have been deployed, the agreement sets forth a set of MIRV counting rules which provide that: (a) all missiles of a type that has been tested with MIRV's shall be counted as MIRV'ed, even if they are deployed with single RV's; and (b) all launchers of a type that has contained or launched MIRV'ed missiles will be counted as MIRV'ed, even if they contain non-MIRV'ed missiles.

Because the Soviet SS-16 ICBM shares certain similarities with the mobile SS-20 IRBM, including a potential capability to be launched by the mobile SS-20 launcher, the Soviet Union has agreed to an outright ban on the deployment, further testing, and production of the SS-16, including the production of component parts unique to the SS-16.

Both nations are required by the treaty to notify the other side in advance of certain ICBM test launches.

Both nations will provide figures on their own strategic offensive forces as part of an agreed data base.

The treaty provides a mechanism for promptly considering any ambiguous situations that may arise in the future and for overseeing the orderly implementation of the provisions of SALT II in the U.S.-Soviet Standing Consultative Commission (SCC). This body is designed to provide a forum in which either nation may raise matters of concern regarding the SALT process. It has worked well as the established means of monitoring the implementation of the SALT I agreements and in providing a continuing forum for further discussions between the two sides with respect to these agreements.

The treaty explicitly states that verification will be by "national technical means" belonging to the other side. National technical means include satellites (such as photoreconnaissance satellites), ground-based systems (such as radars which observe missile tests and antennas which collect telemetry), and aircraft-based systems (including optical systems and other sensors). Thus, neither side is dependent on trust to verify compliance with the provisions of the agreement.

The Protocol to the SALT II Treaty

The protocol enters into force at the same time as the treaty, but it will expire at a considerably earlier date—December 31, 1981. It places temporary limitations on certain systems with regard to which the sides could not reach long-term resolution. These limitations are:

The deployment of mobile ICBM launchers and the flight-testing of ICBM's from such launchers are banned. Development and testing of the launchers alone, however, are not restricted.

The flight-testing and deployment of air-to-surface ballistic missiles with ranges over 600 km are banned.

The deployment of ground-launched and sea-launched cruise missiles is limited to cruise missiles not capable of a range of more than 600 kilometers, or about 350 miles.

There are no other restrictions on the development or flight-testing of ground- and sea-launched cruise missiles, and the 600-kilometer deployment limitations will expire before the United States will be ready to deploy these systems. There are no limitations in the protocol on the range, development, flight-testing, or deployment of air-launched cruise missiles. These weapons will be an important future addition to our existing force of long-range, heavy bombers, and airplanes equipped with long-range, air-launched cruise missiles are included in the 1,320 aggregate of the treaty.

Acronyms

ABM: anti-ballistic missile
ALCM: air-launched cruise missile
ASBM: air-to-surface ballistic missile
ASW: anti-submarine warfare
CM: cruise missile
FBS: forward-based systems
FRODS: functionally-related observable differences
GLCM: ground-launched cruise missile
HB: heavy bomber
ICBM: intercontinental ballistic missile
IRBM: intermediate-range ballistic missile
kt: kiloton
MIRV: multiple, independently-targetable reentry vehicle
MLBM: modern, large ballistic missile

MRBM: medium-range ballistic missile
MRV: multiple reentry vehicle
mt: megaton
MW/CM: multiple-warhead cruise missile
MX: missile experimental
NTM: national technical means
ODs: observable differences
PBV: post-boost vehicle
RV: reentry vehicle
SALT: Strategic Arms Limitation Talks
SAM: surface-to-air missile
SCC: Standing Consultative Commission
SLBM: submarine-launched ballistic missile
SLCM: sea-launched cruise missile
SNDV: strategic nuclear delivery vehicle
SRAM: short-range attack missile
SSBN: nuclear-powered ballistic missile submarine

U.S. and Soviet Strategic Offensive Force Levels

	1 January 1979	
	U.S.	USSR
Operational ICBM Launchers [1,2]	1,054	1,400
Operational SLBM Launchers [1,2,3]	656	950
Long-range Bombers [4]		
Operational [5]	348	150
Others [6]	221	0
Variants [7]	0	120
Force Loadings [8]		
Weapons (Warheads)	9,200	5,000

1 Includes on-line missile launchers as well as those in construction, in overhaul, repair, conversion, and modernization.

2 Does not include test and training launchers, but does include launchers at test sites that are thought to be part of the operational force.

3 Includes launchers on all nuclear-powered submarines and, for the Soviets, operational launchers for modern SLBMs on G-class diesel submarines.

4 Excludes, for the U.S.: 3 B-1 prototypes and 68 FB-111s; for the USSR: BACKFIREs.

5 Includes deployed, strike-configured aircraft only.

6 Includes, for U.S., B-52s used for miscellaneous purposes and those in reserve, mothballs or storage.

7 Includes for USSR: BISON tankers, BEAR ASW aircraft, and BEAR reconnaissance aircraft. U.S. tankers (641 KC-135s) do not use B-52 airframes and are not included.

8 Total force loadings reflect those independently-targetable weapons associated with the total operational ICBMs, SLBMs and long-range bombers.

The Joint Statement of Principles

SALT II is one part of a continuing process of arms control negotiations between the United States and the Soviet Union. This fact is reflected in the joint statement of principles and basic guidelines for subsequent negotiations, which declares that the two sides have agreed to work for further reductions and for further qualitative limitations on their ... and to attempt to re... included in the prot... In addition, it is expl... side may raise any oth... in the SALT III negot...

Backfire

The Soviet Union has undertaken commitments not to increase the rate of production of the Backfire bomber above its current rate and to limit upgrading of the capabilities of this aircraft. The freeze on the Backfire production rate at its current level means that the Soviets are committed not to produce more than 30 Backfires per year. The United States considers the obligations set forth on Backfire as essential to the integrity of the obligations of the treaty as a whole. The commitments by the Soviet Union regarding Backfire have the same legal force as the rest of th... SALT II agreement. Thus, if the ... Union were to violate these com... ments, the United States could wi... draw from the treaty.